On the Trail of Britain's
Fairy Folk

Published by VisitBritain Publishing

VisitBritain Publishing
Thames Tower, Blacks Road, London W6 9EL

First published 2007

© British Tourist Authority (trading as VisitBritain) with Susanna Geoghegan Gift Publishing Consultancy 2007

ISBN 978 0 7095 8423 0

A CIP catalogue record of this book is available from the British Library

Designed and produced for VisitBritain Publishing by Susanna Geoghegan Gift Publishing Consultancy
Publishing Manager for VisitBritain: Jane Collinson
Text: Complete Editions
Map illustrations: Martin Impey
Picture research: Rebecca Barley
Cover design: Peter Wilkinson
Contents design: Chris Hayden

Printed in Malta

visit**Britain**™

Contents

The Little People of Britain

The British countryside is permeated with sites associated with the Fairy Folk, the Hidden People, the Little People. From misty Scottish glens and deep Welsh waters, to the wild moors and isolated coves of Cornwall, the worlds of the Little People and their human neighbours have, according to local legend, frequently come into contact with one another over the centuries – many times for good, but more often it seems for mischief or mayhem.

The Little People of Britain have a diverse pedigree, which stretches far back in the national psyche and which has been recorded in folklore and local legend for approaching 800 years – they are the magical and elusive creatures of cautionary tales and horror stories, of nursery rhymes, of fireside and bedtime stories and, more often than not, of nightmares. They have preyed upon, occasionally given assistance to and been spied upon by their human neighbours. There are sites associated with them throughout the country, a selection of which feature in this book.

Fairies, goblins, pixies, elves, gnomes, and brownies, to use some of the more familiar names by which the Little People are known, frequent a variety of dwelling places: hills and mountains, mounds (both natural and man-made), standing stones, outcrops of rocks, caves and other natural features. There are reports linking Little People with woods and individual trees. A considerable number of the chosen habitats are watery: wells or springs, lakes or pools, rivers or streams. Certain man-made structures are associated with the Little People as well, among them: prehistoric burial mounds, stone crosses, mines, holes and tunnels – all of which imply a link between the Little People and the dead, with Fairyland often being associated with the Underworld.

Ancient as many of these stories are, the sites associated with them retain a timeless wonder that visitors can still enjoy and savour today. *On The Trail of Britain's Fairy Folk* will lead you to many such places , each of which has a strong association with or has inspired tales of fateful encounters between the Little People and mortals. You too will discover that even today many of these sites retain a sense of mystery and magic.

Each chapter takes you on the trail of a particular site and its fairy legend, before describing other places you can visit within the vicinity. Charming, hand-drawn maps show the location of the main site and a highlighted description sets the scene. More practical information to help plan your visit is given in notes on how to get to all the locations described in the chapter, plus useful contact details and web addresses. The book is illustrated throughout with many evocative photographs and enchanting illustrations.

The imposing façade of Dunvegan Castle at sunset

The Fairy Flag of Dunvegan Castle

Fairies of the Isle of Skye and the west of Scotland

MacLeod chiefs have ruled their clan from its ancestral home at Dunvegan Castle on the Isle of Skye since the 13th century, and throughout its turbulent history Dunvegan has housed the clan's most treasured possession: Am Bratach Sith or the Fairy Flag. Today this hangs in the castle's elegant 18th century drawing room, in a gilt frame and protected behind glass, for in times gone by pieces were cut from it by those seeking to acquire for themselves a little of its fabled magic.

Over the centuries a number of legends have arisen about the origins of the flag and how it found its way to Dunvegan. However, one fact is immediately evident on first seeing this tattered fragment of ancient light brown cloth, which contrasts so markedly with the refined Georgian setting where it is on display: Am Bratach Sith is very, very old. In fact, the Fairy Flag is quite possibly 1000 years older than the medieval keep in which it and the drawing room are now housed!

When an expert on ancient textiles informed the then clan chief in the early part of the 20th century that the 'flag' had probably originated in the Middle East in the 4th to 7th centuries AD, Sir Reginald MacLeod of MacLeod replied politely, 'Mr Wace, you

The Bratach Sith, or Fairy Flag, which now hangs in Dunvegan Castle's elegant 18th century drawing room

may believe that, but I know that it was given to my ancestor by the fairies.'

Although exactly which ancestor received it from which fairy has been a source of myth and legend down the centuries.

Two accounts associate the Fairy Flag with the infant heir of the clan MacLeod. In one version, the Lady of MacLeod was spinning yarn when she heard singing in the room where her baby son was asleep. Leaving her spinning wheel, she went to find out who was singing and discovered a little woman in a long green gown, wrapping the baby in a silken banner and singing a spell, which has been passed down as the Fairy Lullaby:

Ho-ro veel-a-vok, bone and flesh of me,
Ho-ro veel-a-vok, blood and pith of me,
Skin like falling snow, green thy mail coat,
Live thy steeds be, dauntless thy following.

'God save us!' cried out poor Lady MacLeod in her terror, 'I am the mother of yon child!'

And the little woman, hearing the Lord's name, immediately vanished. However, the fairy banner remained behind and it became the custom to sing over the chief's children to keep them safe. Indeed, for many generations only nurses who could sing the Fairy Lullaby were employed at Dunvegan Castle.

A similar tale tells of a night when celebrations were being held in the castle. This time it was the nurse who put the chief's little heir in his cradle in the Fairy Tower, before slipping down to the great hall to join in the fun. While she was away, the legend goes, the baby became restless and kicked off his bedding. With his nurse still absent, fairies came to comfort him and wrapped him in a silken shawl to keep him warm.

When his nurse returned, she found the baby in

his fairy wrap and carried him back down to the festivities, so that everyone could see it. As she entered, the hall was mysteriously filled with the sound of unseen singers singing the Fairy Lullaby.

A further version of the legend tells the story of a fairy who married a MacLeod chief and was permitted to live with him for 20 years, before returning to Fairyland. Their parting was a source of great sorrow to both the chief and his fairy wife, who took leave of him at the Fairy Bridge, three miles from Dunvegan. As a parting gift, she gave her husband Am Bratach Sith, telling him that when he was hard pressed in battle, unfurling it would bring a host of armed men to fight alongside him.

Belief in the power of Am Bratach Sith to protect the MacLeod clan in times of danger has been passed down from generation to generation and remains strong among MacLeods the world over. During the Second World War many clansmen serving in the armed forces reputedly carried photographs of the Fairy Flag.

In the dark days of 1940, when invasion of these islands loomed, the clan chief himself is said to have offered to bring the flag from Skye to the White Cliffs of Dover, where he was prepared to unfurl it once more to drive back Hitler's armada. This would have been an act of selfless generosity on his part, for according to legend, the protective powers of the flag will only work three times – and it has already been called on twice in its history to save clansmen in peril. On both occasions (in 1490 and 1520), when the MacLeods were fighting for their lives against overwhelming numbers of MacDonalds, the Fairy Flag turned almost certain defeat into stunning victory.

Although the flag was not unfurled as such, when fire swept through Dunvegan in 1939, many people were convinced that it had prevented the castle from being destroyed completely. Now Am Bratach Sith hangs serenely in the fine drawing room, venerated and revered – its saving power still held in the deepest respect.

Between Dunvegan and Edinbane, at the foot of the Waternish peninsula, where the B886 branches north from the A850, lies an abandoned bridge beside the modern road. This is the Fairy Bridge – the very place where the chief of the MacLeods parted from his fairy wife when she returned to her people.

Travelling round the coast to the north of the island brings you to Duntulm Bay. If the visibility is good look across towards Tulm Island and then beyond,

A stunning view of Tulm Island across Duntulm Bay

and you may just make out Fladda, a small island once held to be the sacred Fladda of the Ocean, also known as Tir-nan-Og, the Island of Perpetual Youth. This was a fairy realm where the inhabitants lived an idyllic life of feasting, music and dance in a land where it was always summer.

Across the narrow strip of water dividing the Isle of Skye from the mainland Bernera and then round the waters of Glenelg Bay, you come to Glenelg, the site of another memorable fairy encounter. A mythical Celtic warrior called Fionn was hunting here, when his hounds put up a hind and gave chase. Being magical hounds they soon realised the deer was bewitched. Fionn spared her life and she turned into a lovely, fairy woman. Later she gave birth to their son Ossian, who became a legendary warrior and bard, at Arisaig, which lies further south on the Road to the Isles, opposite the Island of Eigg.

~ON THE TRAIL~

Built atop The Rock on the shores of Loch Dunvegan, with its crenellated walls and towers reflecting in the still waters below, Dunvegan Castle would look perfectly at home in a fairytale landscape. You certainly feel you are stepping into another world as you pass behind the castle's stern exterior and discover a beautifully elegant and comfortable home.

This inviting interior was mainly created by the 23rd Chief of the Clan MacLeod – known as The General – in the late 18th century. The large windows, which replaced the former defensive slits, now let the light flood in, revealing the full transformation by The General and his architect of this medieval shell into a suite of elegant rooms, which could have easily graced a fashionable mansion in the capital.

In the drawing room, between two windows that look out across the rolling waves of the sea, hangs the castle's most precious relic, Am Bratach Sith or the Fairy Flag. The silk from which it is made is believed to have been yellow originally but is now pale and translucent – adding credence to the legend of its fairy origin. Its great age has left it extremely fragile and it now hangs behind glass to preserve it and its protective spell for generations of MacLeods to come.

Locations to visit

DUNVEGAN CASTLE:

Isle of Skye

IV55 8WF Scotland

Tel: 01470 521206

Fax: 01470 521205

Website: www.dunvegancastle.com

FAIRY BRIDGE:

At the southern end of the Waternish peninsula, beside the B886 which branches north from the A850.

DUNTULM BAY:

The bay lies just to the west of the northernmost tip of Skye and can be reached by travelling north from Uig on the A855.

GLENELG AND ARISAIG:

Glenelg can be reached by taking a minor road from the head of Loch Duish before traversing the Mam Ratagan Pass and dropping down to the village beside its own bay.

Arisaig lies on the coast approximately 40 miles west of Fort William on the A830.

The distinctive silhouette of the Fairy Hill or
Doon Hill seen across the River Forth at sunrise

Doon Hill and the Fairy Minister

Fairies of the Trossachs and Breadalbane

In 1685, the people of Aberfoyle, in Perthshire, acquired a new minister. His name was Robert Kirk and he was the seventh and youngest son of James Kirk. Robert had begun his career in an unremarkable way, studying theology at St Andrew's and Edinburgh universities before turning to the cloth. After moving to Aberfoyle he took to walking up nearby Doon Hill every day to take some regular exercise. Again, there was nothing peculiar in the minister taking care of his health.

His work too attracted little comment. The minister of Aberfoyle was involved in translating the Psalter and the Bible into Gaelic – again, nothing especially unusual for a man of his calling. However, it was his next publication, which appeared in 1691, that proved to be very remarkable. *The Secret Commonwealth* was all about 'Elves, Fauns and Fairies': the Sith as they were called in Gaelic. It was a comprehensive description of a hidden, parallel world, generally visible only to the tabhaiser, or seer.

As the book explained, the denizens of the other world lived underground in beautiful houses. They lived far longer than humans, but not for ever. According to Kirk they were not as solid as we are but were formed from 'congealed air' and were of 'a middle nature betwixt man and angel'. Although their homes were located below the surface, they were never far from human dwellings. They wore the same sort of clothing that humans would wear, so, for instance, in Scotland they would wear the plaid. The Sith spoke in clear voices that sounded like whistling. On Quarter Days in particular they moved about in great numbers and those were the days that people with 'the gift' were most likely to see them. Those that did found it a disturbing experience, and were often frightened by what they would suddenly catch sight of. Equally unnerving was Kirk's claim that everyone had a double in the fairy world, which he called a 'co-walker' (what was later to be called a doppelgänger). If this fairy double was seen apart from the human counterpart it foretold that person's imminent death. This belief was very widely held by the local people.

Being a seventh son, Robert Kirk may have had the second sight himself, although, as a man of the cloth and living when he did, he would have been reluctant to admit to this. He was, however, convinced, by the sheer number of stories about the wee folk and the strength of the local people's belief in their

existence, that he was recording a real phenomenon.

Whether he had the sight or not, the end of his story is as mysterious as anything contained in *The Secret Commonwealth*. One May day in 1692 he set out to climb Doon Hill, although whether he knew it or not, it would be for the last time. When he failed to return, his footsteps were retraced by villagers who went in search of him and his body was discovered on the path where he had collapsed and died. Or had he, in fact, died?

The Reverend Robert Kirk is said to have appeared some time later to his cousin, Graham of Duchray, saying that he was not dead but had been taken from the hill by the fairies. (Local people would not have been surprised to hear this – Robert Kirk was paying the price for having revealed the fairies' secrets.) Robert told his cousin that he would appear again at the christening of his, as yet, unborn child. He told

Graham that, when he appeared, he should throw a dagger over the head of the apparition (presumably because fairies have a great dislike of iron) and this would rescue him from the fairy realm. Unfortunately, it turned out that poor Robert had chosen the wrong man to carry out this task. When he appeared as foretold, Graham was so overcome with fear that he failed to do what was required and so Robert remained a prisoner of the fairies ever after.

The path winding up Doon Hill (also known as Fairy Knowe) leads to a solitary pine tree, called the Minister's Pine. It is said that Robert Kirk's spirit is imprisoned in this tree – punishment for daring to reveal to the mortal race secrets that should have remained hidden.

Not far from Aberfoyle lies the Lake of Monteith. Pointing out into the waters of the lake is a finger of land, said to have been formed by fairy folk as they strove to weave a length of rope out of sand. They had been given this impossible task by the Earl of Monteith, who is said to have released them into the mortal world after reading a fairy book. To rid himself of the fairies, the Earl eventually gifted them a meeting place on a mountain to the north-west. The fairies are said to still meet on the side of Ben Venue to this day, at a place called Coire nan Uruisgean.

The whole area around Loch Tay was the haunt of fairy cattle, which grazed beside, or even in, its waters. Killin, at the south-western end of the loch, is home to the Breadalbane Folklore Centre, which contains displays and exhibitions about life in the area in bygone days and descriptions of the many legends associated with the whole area of Loch Tay and Rannoch Moor.

Visible to the north is Schiehallion, its name a corruption of the Gaelic name which translates as 'The Fairy Hill of the Caledonians'. The mountain's

View of Black Mount on Rannoch Moor

distinctive pointed shape is visible from miles around, brooding above Loch Rannoch. It is the site of visitations by a spectral dog and on its slopes is a fairy well. The fairies who lived there would grant wishes and cure illness. On May Day the locals would visit it, the girls wearing white dresses, offering flowers and other little gifts to the wee folk.

People who lived in the area of Schiehallion and Rannoch Moor regarded it as an eerie and haunted land. Several described being followed by the shadow of a great dog as they walked on the slopes of the mountain. Others reported seeing fairies, and the waters of Loch Rannoch were well known as the home of kelpies – fairy horses that lived in water. If you encountered a kelpie it would try to get you to ride it. Once you had climbed on, the kelpie would then dash back into its watery home, carrying you with it. Kelpies were very strong and wild and only if you could get possession of their magic bridle would you have control over them. Many years ago, a man walking beside the waters of Loch Rannoch found an exquisitely decorated bridle and naturally assumed it belonged to a kelpie. He kept the bridle in the belief that it would give him power over the fabulous beast.

~ON THE TRAIL~

Aberfoyle is described as the Gateway to the Trossachs, once a wild frontier land before its shimmering lochs, deep-cut wooded glens and craggy mountain tops confirmed its status as Scotland's premier holiday region. Once a quiet highland community, the attractions became similarly known to the population at large following the publication of Sir Walter Scott's *The Lady of the Lake*. He wrote it while staying in Aberfoyle and drew heavily on the glorious scenery surrounding it for inspiration.

The village of Aberfoyle lies within Loch Lomond and the Trossachs National Park amidst soaring mountains and deep, cool lochs. Those exploring fairy stories will be drawn to one of the perhaps less spectacular peaks, Doon Hill, to trace poor Robert Kirk's last walk. The path leads from his church, now lying in picturesque ruins, and winds its way through the trees towards the top. The strange atmosphere of the place is often remarked upon and intensifies as you approach the clearing where a huge pine tree stands – this is the Minister's Pine. It stands alone and is highly visible from the surrounding landscape. Around it the other trees are hung with ribbons that flutter in the passing breeze and bear messages politely addressed to the fairies, asking for favours to be granted and for wishes to come true. Be sure to take a piece of coloured cloth to leave your own wish for the fairies of Doon Hill.

Back in the churchyard, searching among the memorials you will find Robert Kirk's tomb. It is a large slab lying on the ground, bearing an inscription written in Latin that states the bare facts – his work as a minister and the date of his death. Look for the carvings of a thistle, the shepherd's crook (the emblem of a shepherd of souls) and a dagger – perhaps the one that Graham of Duchray should have hurled over Robert's spectral head to release him from the fairies' spell.

Locations to visit

DOON HILL:

From the car park in Aberfoyle cross the bridge over the river Forth until you reach the Old Kirk. The path to Doon Hill continues as a forestry track to Gartmore and is waymarked 'The Fairy Trail'.

LOCH TAY AND THE BREADALBANE FOLKLORE CENTRE:

Loch Tay lies between Pitlochry in the east and the Loch Lomond and The Trossachs National Park in the south-west. The A827 runs along its northern shore and a minor road runs along the southern shore. The two roads meet at Killin at the Loch's western end. Breadalbane Folklore Centre is located at Killin.

SCHIEHALLION:

Schiehallion lies to the south-east of Loch Rannoch. A minor road between Kinloch Rannoch and the B846, south of Tummel Bridge, passes beneath it.

RANNOCH MOOR AND LOCH RANNOCH:

Rannoch Moor is to the east of the A82 that runs from Bridge of Orchy to Glencoe. Alternatively, trains from Glasgow or Fort William run to the remote Rannoch Station. Loch Rannoch is to the north of Loch Tay and can be reached by taking the B8019 from Killiecrankie to Tummel Bridge and then the B846.

Overlooking the Firth of Forth with a view to the south of Ailsa Craig, the majestic castle of Culzean sits perched atop the 100-foot cliff top

The Fairy Boy of Culzean Castle

Fairies of southern Scotland and Edinburgh

Every inch a fairy castle in appearance, Culzean Castle was the setting for one of southern Scotland's most popular fairy tales. The story dates from centuries ago, a time when the castle was a simple stone fortress and when the owners of Culzean Castle were known thereabouts as the Lairds o' Co' – a name given to Culzean after the co's (coves) in the rocks at the base of the castle.

The story tells how one morning the Laird o' Co' received a strange visitor: a very small boy, who presented himself to the laird bearing an equally small wooden cup. The boy begged the owner of the castle for some ale to give to his mother, who was sick and in need of nourishment. Touched with pity by the pathetic figure he cut, the laird kindly obliged and sent the tiny boy happily away with the castle butler, with instructions that he should fill the minuscule cup.

The butler had a barrel of ale on tap, only half of which had been used. Carefully holding the boy's cup beneath the tap, he turned it a fraction to let out a few drops – enough to fill the cup, he thought, but not so much that it would spill over and waste the barrel's precious contents. However, more than a few drops were required and the butler tentatively opened the tap a little more, careful not to overfill the cup held between his fingers. However, even this increased rate of flow failed to send the ale racing to the brim of the cup. So the butler opened the tap further and further until a steady flow of ale poured into the tiny cup with no sign of it reaching the top.

To the butler's astonishment, ale flowed from the barrel into the little boy's cup until the barrel was empty. Half a barrel of fine ale had been poured into the cup and still it had not been filled. The butler did not feel inclined to broach a fresh barrel of ale, but the little boy reminded him of the laird's orders that his cup should be filled. Still uncertain, the butler went to the laird to explain the extraordinary events taking place in the cellar. But his master repeated his instruction that the boy's cup had to be filled – adding that the butler could use all the ale in the cellar if it was needed. Obeying his instructions, the castle butler opened a second barrel and just as the first drop plopped into the cup, it was full.

The little boy thanked the butler and then went in search of the laird to thank him too before hurrying away to offer the ale to his mother.

Several years passed, and the Laird o' Co' was overseas fighting in Flanders when he was taken prisoner and sentenced to die a felon's death. His situation looked hopeless. Hundreds of miles from home, he found himself locked in a strongly barricaded prison with no hope of escape and facing a grisly death the following morning. Resigned to his fate, he was contemplating his last night on earth when the doors of his prison miraculously burst open. Standing there was the small boy, who now addressed the laird:

Laird o' Co', Rise an' go.

The prisoner needed no second bidding and fled his prison cell. Once outside, the little boy told him to climb onto his shoulders. Realising perhaps that his tiny saviour was a fairy, the laird did as he was told and in a flash found himself deposited outside the gate of his own home, far, far away at Culzean, where he and the fairy had first met.

The laird barely had time to express his gratitude when the fairy vanished, but not before he had told the Laird o' Co': *Ae guid turn deserves anither.*

Tak ye that for being sae kind to my auld mither.

Originally discovered in a cleft below Arthur's Seat in Edinburgh, these mysterious little 'fairy coffins' are now on exhibition at the Museum of Scotland

Cross Scotland from the Firth of Clyde to the Firth of Forth and two of Edinburgh's seven hills have strong fairy connections. In 1836 an extraordinary find was made in a cleft below Arthur's Seat. Hidden there, over a period spanning many years it appeared, was a cache of 'fairy coffins', delicately made and containing dressed wooden effigies. Their purpose remains a mystery and today they are securely housed in the Museum of Scotland.

Years ago it was believed that Calton Hill, another of Edinburgh's seven hills, contained a gateway set into the hillside leading to fairyland. Only certain people could find it and enter, notably a ten-year-old boy who came to public attention in the mid-1660s. He seemed to have 'the second sight' which he claims was given to him by the fairies of Calton Hill. He went every

Thursday night and entered the fairy realm through a great gateway. He played the drums whilst the fairies danced and for this he was rewarded with his unique powers.

Lying in the border country south of Edinburgh, Earlston in Berwickshire was once home of Thomas Learmont of Ercildoune who built a small castle there in the 13th century. He became better known as Thomas the Rhymer; the castle keep is called Rhymer's Tower. He too had a reputation as a 'seer' or prophet, having been granted these special powers by the Queen of Elfland, whom he was said to have seduced and lived with in her magical kingdom for seven years.

Close to the village of Ednam, near Kelso, stands a Pictish burial mound known locally as The Piper's Grave. It takes its name from the sad fate of a piper, who managed to get inside the mound in an attempt to learn the fairies' beautiful tunes. He should have taken a charm with him to guard against enchantment, as without one he was unable to find his way out again and remained trapped forever underground. It is said that music can still be heard coming from the mound.

A happier tale is centred on a hill near Hawick called Rubers Law. It was here that a man on his way to Hawick sheep fair came upon a fairy woman and her baby. It was a very cold day and the fairy had nothing warm to wrap her baby in. The man stopped and gave her the plaid from his shoulders before continuing on to Hawick. When he got to the market the first thing he noticed was the low cost of the sheep he bought. Such good fortune stayed with him thereafter and he enjoyed considerable prosperity for the rest of his life.

Testimony to the malign intervention of the Buggane the ruin of St Trinians still sits roofless and unused

The Buggane of St. Trinian's Chapel

Fairies of the Isle of Man

Nearly 800 years ago some monks came to the foot of Greeba Mountain on the Isle of Man and chose a pleasant meadow as the site for a new chapel. The original building was even enlarged a while later but, at some point in its history, it fell into disuse and the islanders tell an extraordinary story explaining how this happened.

Local legend holds that there lived up on the slopes of Greeba Mountain a very disagreeable creature called a buggane. It was a kind of shape-shifting goblin who had a general dislike for churches and who was particularly irritated by the sounds of bells and singing rising to its lair from St Trinian's chapel. Then there came a time when the chapel needed to be re-roofed, but every time work started on the repair, the workmen would arrive in the morning to find beams and rafters tossed off the walls and lying scattered in the grass around the building. The buggane had come down at night and wrecked the previous day's work in a successful attempt to scare away the builders. Sometimes he would cause the havoc himself, sometimes he summoned up a storm to tear off the new roof.

The parishioners got together and decided to go ahead with one last attempt to roof the chapel. They had the feeling that if it stayed on for one night it would stay on for good. They were further encouraged to try once more by a little tailor called Timothy who lived in the neighbourhood. He wasn't very well off and saw an opportunity to improve his lot by wagering the others that he would spend the night in the chapel and ensure the new roof remained in place. Furthermore, he undertook to make a pair of trousers during the course of the night. His wager was accepted, as it seemed no one had a better plan.

The builders set to work again the next day and managed to raise the roof before the sun set. They waited anxiously for Timothy to arrive and, as soon as he did, they hurried away to reach their homes before it became really dark. The little tailor entered the church and put down his pack whilst he lit some candles. He then took out the things he needed to make his pair of trousers, settled down and began to sew. He worked quickly because he needed to finish the work before morning, in order to win the bet he had made with the villagers.

Timothy didn't really believe in bugganes and had felt quite confident when he made his offer at the meeting that there would be a perfectly normal explanation for the disturbances at the chapel. However, as he worked in the pale light of the candles and listened to the wind rising outside he began to feel uneasy. He became aware of unearthly howls and shrieks, distant at first, but each one louder and nearer than the last. This made him concentrate on his work more fiercely, struggling to make his fingers fly and not tremble too much.

Suddenly the door of the chapel crashed open and a huge, shadowy figure lurched inside. It was some kind of animal, covered with coarse hair, with cloven hooves that rang on the stone floor. Its burning eyes fell on little Timothy, who had just enough time to put the last stitch in the trousers before jumping up and throwing himself out of the nearest window which he had opened as a precaution. Clutching the trousers to him, he stumbled across the churchyard as fast as his legs would carry him. From behind him he heard the beast bellowing. There was a tremendous crash as the new roof fell to the ground. Unable to help himself, the little tailor turned to see the buggane in pursuit. As he watched in disbelief, the foul thing tore its own head off and hurled it at Timothy before collapsing to the ground. The head rolled and bounced towards the tailor and, by the time it came to a stop at his feet, it had turned to stone.

When presented with the new trousers, and in appreciation of Timothy's bravery, the parishioners honoured the wager they had made with him. His experiences had been so terrifying and the commotion of the night so great, that no one had the heart to try to re-roof the chapel again. So there it lies in the little meadow, roofless still and open to heaven and the elements just as the buggane had left it.

Passing the Fairy Bridge, signposted on the A5

The ruin of St Trinian's which sits sheltering under the shadow of the rocky Greeba Mountain

Be sure to give a polite greeting to 'themselves' as you cross over the Fairy Bridge

between Douglas and Castletown, be sure to greet the fairy folk politely; the 'quaer fellas' or 'themselves' (as they're known locally) do not take kindly to discourteous travellers. Various sites have been given for the Fairy Bridge over the last 100 years as new roads have been built, but for many the original, and 'real', fairy bridge is hidden away and only accessible to walkers along a winding, woodland path in Kewaigue, off the old Castletown road.

A warning of what can happen to humans who upset fairies comes from the pretty coastal village of

Laxey, on the east coast of the Isle of Man, north of Douglas. Here a local farmer greatly offended the fairies when he came upon them when drunk and swore at them. First his livestock died, then 40 days later he died as well.

At Glen Roy, near Laxey, lies Nikkesen's Pool, named after Nikkesen the fairy who inhabited the pool and had the dubious habit of emerging from it in the guise of a beautiful young man. He seduced the local girls and took them back to his pool. The only time they were seen again by their grieving families was on clear nights when the moon was full. If they came to the hill above the pool they would see the heartless sprite bring the girls out and lead them in a dance in the meadow.

Across the island, at Orrisdale, near Kirk Michael on the west coast, stands a prehistoric site where fairies like to hold their feasts. On one such occasion they were passing round a silver goblet full of magic potion when a mortal stumbled upon the party. They offered him the cup, but he knew that he would become enchanted if he drank from it and so he emptied the contents on the ground, whereupon the fairies disappeared and left the man holding the empty goblet, which was presented to the church to be sanctified as a communion cup. Even though the church attempted to sanctify the cup, anyone drinking from it still descended into madness.

On around the coast and then inland to Andreas, in the north of the Isle of Man, Maughold church was built on the site of one the earliest Christian establishments on the island: a Celtic monastery, founded there in the 7th century. The 'crosshouse' in the churchyard contains an important collection of pre-Norse cross slabs, or memorials, found on the island. It is strange, therefore, that such an ancient Christian site is also said, according to legend, to be a place where fairies used to emerge from an underground passage, having travelled from the nearby earthwork of Shan Cashtal to Maughold churchyard.

Maughold churchyard

~On The Trail~

The roofless, ruined walls, empty windows and doorways of St Trinian's chapel still stand today much as you imagine they must have done after the terrified tailor fled before the rampaging buggane. Known as Keeil Vrisht, the Broken Church, in the Manx Dialect, St Trinian's chapel can be found in a field a little less than a mile south-west of the village of Crosby.

Greeba Mountain, the buggane's rocky lair, rises behind – from the summit of which, on a clear day, you can glimpse the outline of the Irish coast across the water to the west.

Standing among the chapel ruins today, you may hear what sounds very like the roar of a terrifying monster as high-speed motorcycles scream past the chapel ruins during the Isle of Man's famous TT Races.

Locations to visit

ST TRINIAN'S CHAPEL:

The chapel lies in a field beside the A1, ¾ mile west of Crosby.

FAIRY BRIDGE:

The A5 between Douglas and Castletown crosses the Fairy Bridge just south of Santon. The 'real' Fairy Bridge is no more than a 15-minute walk from the Old Castleton Road, near a footpath from Kewaigue to Oak Hill. This path is signposted a short distance up the hill, opposite Kewaigue School.

NIKKESEN'S POOL:

The pool is located in the Awin Ruy stream near its junction with the Glen Roy River. Glen Roy is at the northern end of Laxey Glen.

FAIRY HILL:

This tumulus lies four hundred yards north-east of Orrisdale House, near Kirk Michael, on the west coast of the island.

SHAN CASHTAL BARROW:

Near the village of Andreas, in the north of the island.

The rushing waters of Janet's Foss, near Malham, one of Charles Kingsley's key inspirations.

Malham Tarn and the Water-Babies

Fairies of the Yorkshire Dales

In 1863 the writer Charles Kingsley visited the Yorkshire Dales and was captivated by its wild, dramatic scenery, which no doubt reminded him of the Dartmoor landscapes where he had lived as a boy.

One of the places he stayed at was the Tarn House at Malham, overlooking Malham Tarn: a natural upland lake which acts as a focal point for some of the most dramatic limestone scenery found in upland Britain. In Kingsley's day, Malham was as much a walker's paradise as it is now and in reply to one visitor's enquiry about the black streaks down the nearby limestone cliffs of Malham Cove, Kingsley jokingly replied that a chimney-sweep must have fallen over them.

Whether or not his enquirer remembered Kingsley's quip, it lodged in the writer's memory, from where it would emerge not long after his return to his family, mingled with folk tales and fairy stories that he had encountered from his stay in the Dales. In Kingsley's creative hands, these disparate elements were brought together to create one of his best-loved stories, to which he gave the tiltle: *The Water-Babies, A Fairy Tale for a Land-Baby* – the 'land-baby' of the title was Kingsley's youngest child, Grenville Arthur.

The early chapters of the book are set in the rugged countryside around Harthover Fell and Lewthwaite Crag, creations of Kingsley's which bear remarkable parallels with the Pennine landscapes that had inspired him during his time at Malham. Here, Tom, an orphan chimney-sweep, is employed by his cruel foul-mouthed master, Grimes, to climb up flues and brush down the soot. On a visit to the baronial home of Sir John Harthover, Tom's life takes an unexpected turn and he finds himself escaping across the moors and down a steep limestone cliff (very like those at Malham). Even when his safety is secured, Tom is exhausted and feverish. Walking to the banks of a nearby river, he strips off his clothes and gratefully sinks beneath the surface to refresh himself. His physical body drowns in the river, but Tom is reborn in a new form – a water-baby, tiny, amphibious and immortal. In other words, he becomes a fairy.

This metamorphosis introduces Kingsley's water-baby to water creatures, with whom he is able to converse, and to a cast of fairies who instruct him in the workings of the world in which he finds himself. In writing the book, Kingsley attacked not only the appalling inhumanity of child labour, but also what he regarded as the wholly unwarranted fashion in children's books of the day, which rejected fairy stories in favour of factual books of instruction. In contrast, *The Water-Babies* is purely a story of the imagination, presenting a vivid, invented world of magical beings and written to excite and capture his young reader's imagination.

A careful and articulate observer of the natural world (particularly underwater and undersea life), Kingsley captures the spirit of the breathtaking scenery around Malham, at the heart of which lies the beautiful but mysterious tarn which first kindled his imaginative impulse.

Chief among the inspirations for Kingsley's story would have been Janet's Foss, near Malham. Janet, or Jennet, was the queen of the local fairies and was said to have lived in a cave behind the foss, or waterfall.

Ten miles to the south-east of Malham stands 'The Barden Triangle', defining an area around the head of Lower Wharfedale well known for supernatural phenomena. Troller's Gill near Appletreewick is particularly spooky. Once the haunt of a terrible barguest, a huge hound, that as late as 1881 claimed a victim, it is also frequented by all sorts of sprites, mostly disagreeable. The area was said to be inhabited by man-eating trolls who dropped rocks on unsuspecting wayfarers or lured them to their fate by trickery. Today's visitors to the Gill are still often unsettled by its strange eeriness.

Elbolton Hill, near Burnsall, was renowned for fairies. One man reported seeing them dancing one night and was so caught up in the merriment he called to them, offering to sing a song for them. But the dancing fairy folk promptly vanished.

~On The Trail~

Malham Tarn feels and looks every inch a lake of fairy enchantment and wonder, surrounded as it is by the stunning, but sometimes bleak, scenery of rolling hills embroidered by dry-stone walls and patterned with 'pavements' of exposed limestone.

Add to this the awe-inspiring amphitheatre of cliffs of nearby Malham Cove, rising above almost 100 metres, and the rumbling waterfalls so beloved of fairy folk, and you could be transported into the pages of Kingsley's tale of sprites and water-babies.

Today, the Pennine Way and the growing popularity of fell walking attract increasing numbers of admiring visitors. Seen early in the morning, or in the fading shadows of the evening, when the land is at rest, there are few more compelling vistas in England. Wild and largely untamed, there is a raw majesty to be seen in the still waters of the tarn and the heather-clad fells that surround it. And if you are willing to rise early and are prepared to endure weather conditions that usually keep other visitors at home, you will truly experience the spirit of this awe-inspiring landscape, which so captivated Charles Kingsley.

Locations to visit

MALHAM:

Malham is to the north-west of Skipton and the minor road leading to it branches off the A65, near Cargrave. Walk north along the Pennine Way to reach Malham Cove and Malham Tarn.

JANET'S FOSS:

Janet's Foss is near Goredale Scar. A footpath leads to it from the village of Malham, starting at Malham Smithy and following Malham Beck.

THE BARDEN TRIANGLE:

Appletreewick lies just to the east of the B6160, about eight miles north-east of Skipton. Troller's Gill is a limestone ravine in the valley of Trollerdale below Simon Seat.

Elbolton Hill overlooks the village of Thorpe, some six miles north of Skipton, between the B6265 and the B6160.

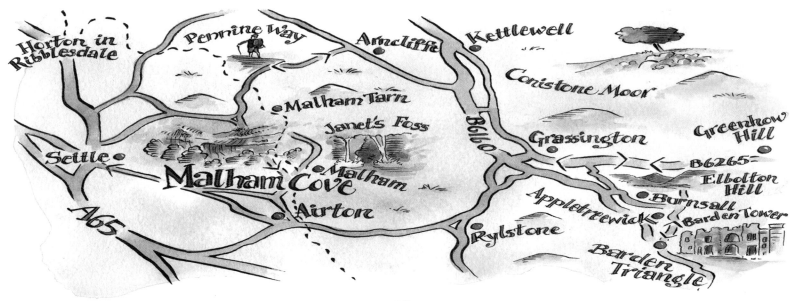

The 10-year-old Frances Griffiths photographed with the 'fairies' by Elsie Wright in July 1917

The Cottingley Fairies

Yorkshire's most famous fairies

The photograph of Frances Griffiths and the so-called 'Leaping Fairy' taken in August 1920

In 1917 Europe was still engulfed in a war characterised by its appalling tally of casualties and by battlefields where large tracts of land were transformed into mud-filled, cratered wastes. In contrast, two young girls who lived at 31 Lynwood Terrace, in the Yorkshire town of Cottingley, near Bingley, had discovered a haven of peace far removed from such horrors and had spent that spring and summer playing in a 'fairy glen' behind the row of houses forming the terrace. Elsie Wright was the older of the two and her constant companion was Frances Griffiths, a cousin from South Africa who was living with the Wright family at the time.

For many of us, their story will bring back childhood memories of warm days spent with a close friend, immersed in a magical world conjured up by woods, fields and streams. Elsie and Frances enjoyed the freedom of the holidays to roam through their particular patch of countryside, made all the more special because of the presence of the industrial heartland nearby. The two young girls found imaginary friends there to play with, as well as each other. Or so Elsie's mother and father thought, when the two of them kept chattering at mealtimes about the little people they had met – especially those living beside a waterfall on Cottingley Beck, shaded by trees in the fairy glen behind the house.

Elsie's father was an eminently practical man, being one of a new breed of technicians – a qualified electrical engineer. As the girls continued to insist that they had met real fairies in the glen, an exasperated Mr Wright finally allowed them to take his camera to capture the little people of on film. If he thought that would put an end to their 'nonsense', he could not have been more wrong.

When Elsie and Frances came back with the camera Arthur Wright took the negative and developed it in his tiny darkroom under the stairs. Slowly images began to appear – first a lovely picture of Frances in a sylvan setting – then other mysterious items that he took to be bits of paper or sandwich wrappers. When fully developed, however, these turned out to be several tiny fairies dancing in front of the little girl. This photograph, and another that the girls produced a short while later of a pixie about to step onto Elsie's hand, were to become an international sensation. Not immediately, though, because Mr and Mrs Wright kept the existence of these photographs a secret within the family. Elsie's father and mother kept challenging the girls to admit that it was all a prank until, in the face of their absolute refusal to do so, Arthur Wright forbade them to use his camera again.

Like many others during those turbulent times of the Great War, his wife had turned to Theosophy and spiritualism to find comfort and some degree of certainty about life after death. In 1919 she attended a lecture about the existence of otherwordly beings such as fairies. In the general discussion that developed afterwards she spoke of her daughter's claims to have met fairies. Before long it was revealed that photographs existed capturing these encounters and the lecturer asked to see them. He was duly amazed by their apparent authenticity; and ripples of interest spread beyond the locality of Cottingley.

Experts in both psychic matters and in photography were drawn in – some hard-nosed investigators becoming convinced that the fairies the girls said they saw and had photographed were absolutely real. Edward Lewis Gardner was one such researcher. He presented a camera each to Elsie and Frances and asked if they could capture more images of their ethereal friends. After he left them to it and returned to London it proceeded to rain for the next two weeks, preventing the girls from going out on their fairy safari; the fairy folk liked to come out when the sun shone. However, on 19 August 1920, Elsie's mother Polly wrote the following to Edward Gardner:

The morning was dull and misty so they did not take any photos until after dinner when 'The mist had cleared away and it was sunny. I went to my sister's for tea and left them to it. When I got back they had only managed two with fairies, I was disappointed.

P.S. She did not take one flying after all'

In fact, three more photographs were taken, one showing Frances looking at a leaping fairy, one of a fairy offering a flower to Elsie and another of fairies standing by a gossamer 'sunbath'.

By now, celebrities were joining the throng of interest and speculation surrounding the girls and their extraordinary story. Sir Arthur Conan Doyle, creator of the famous Baker Street sleuth, Sherlock Holmes, became an ardent supporter of their claims. It was he, with Edward Gardner, who submitted the photographs to *The Strand* magazine for publication in the Christmas edition of 1920. Until then, Conan Doyle had enjoyed a reputation for possessing as keen a mind as Sherlock himself, but many of his admirers now looked askance at his willingness to believe in fairies. He continued, however, to stand by his belief in the Cottingley fairies until his death in 1930.

Elsie and Frances's notoriety gradually faded, but never disappeared. In adult life, Elsie went abroad to live, first in America, then India, and returned to England in the late 1940s. Frances also travelled overseas before settling back in England. Both women remained stubbornly mute on the veracity or otherwise of their celebrated photos. Finally, in a book written in 1983 and also in an article for *The Times*, Frances confessed that the photographs were indeed fakes – conceived as a joke and as a way of 'getting back' at sceptical adults – but the deception had assumed a life and momentum of its own from which it became impossible to withdraw.

Frances held her belief in fairies until her death in 1986 and claimed that the fifth photograph, the one which shows the fairies around a sunbath, was not a fake but records a real sighting. As she explained in later life: 'It was a wet Saturday afternoon and we were just mooching about with our cameras and Elsie had nothing prepared. I saw these fairies building up in the grasses and just aimed the camera and took a photograph.' She always maintained that she and Elsie had seen fairies at the bottom of the garden of 31 Lynwood Terrace.

The photographs created by the two girls touched a nerve in the collective consciousness of British people at the time. Life and society were changing rapidly, scientific knowledge was accelerating and yet carnage was taking place on the battlefields of World War I on an unprecedented scale. Pictures of fairies innocently playing with young girls by a waterfall in a secret setting provided an enchanting alternative to the mechanised world evolving around them.

Travel north-east to the western edge of the North York Moors and you discover a natural, and more ancient, fairy site at Pudding Pie Hill, near Thirsk. This is a prehistoric burial mound, which was reused in Saxon times. Legend says that if you run round the hill nine times then stick a knife in the ground you will be able to hear the fairies, who dwell beneath the hill.

Across the heather-clad moors, riven with steep-sided valleys, lies the ancient port of Whitby, which straddles the mouth of the River Esk where it flows into the North Sea. As well as an important trading, whaling and fishing centre, Whitby was once the heart of the jet jewellery-making industry. Found in abundance locally, jet was believed to provide protection against evil spirits and fairy enchantment, the same as amber – hence jet also being known as 'black amber'. Whitby Museum houses a collection of jet artefacts to ward off evil spirits. The town and its time-worn abbey, dramatically situated on the east cliff overlooking the harbour, also featured in Bram Stoker's classic vampire thriller, *Dracula*.

A few miles up the coast from Whitby are two more well-known haunts for local sprites. At the far end of the beach from the delightful cliff-hugging village of Runswick Bay, there are holes in the cliff called Hob Holes. (A hob is a sort of goblin, mischievous but also helpful.) The Hob Hole inhabitants were reputed to be especially skilled in curing whooping cough. Mothers would take afflicted children along the arc of sand to Hob Holes where they would solemnly recite:

> *Hob Hole Hob,*
> *Hob Hole Hob,*
> *My bairn's got t' cough.*
> *Tak't off! Tak't off!*

A little inland from Runswick are the mysterious Mulgrave Woods, said to be inhabited by a famous bogle called Jeannie. Bogles are not very pleasant goblin-like creatures and are thus best avoided, as the tale of Mulgrave Woods reveals. This tells of a

Sitting dramatically atop the cliffs, Whitby's time-worn abbey overlooks the town and its sheltered harbour

foolhardy farmer who set out to find Jeannie and made his way to the entrance to her cave. He boldly called out to her and, sure enough, she rushed out. However, she turned out to be so hideous and terrifying that the farmer and his horse immediately fled. The horrified farmer made straight for a stream (bogles, like many fairy folk, can't cross water) and spurred his horse over. The pursuing Jeannie reached out and managed to touch the horse, which was sliced in two. But the rider landed on the far side of the stream and survived to tell his terrifying tale.

The 'green children' of Woolpit are still remembered today on the village sign and on the church altar cloth

The Green Children of Woolpit

Fairies of Suffolk

It has always been said that the name of the village of Woolpit comes from the early days of its existence when life was harsh and wild beasts roamed the forests. To defend the settlement from these marauders, trenches were dug to trap them, especially the wolves that might ravish the flocks. The trenches were the wolf pits from which the village later took its name.

It was near the wolf pits that, at some point in the 12th century, two very unusual visitors were discovered. Peasants working in the nearby fields came across two young children, a boy and a girl, huddled together in a distressed state. What made the men who found them stop and stare in amazement was the fact that the children's skin was green. When asked where they came from, they answered in an unknown language.

Thoroughly baffled, the farm workers took the green children to the house of a local squire, Sir Richard de Caine.

It was evident that they were hungry, though when they were offered food they refused to eat it and began to cry. At that moment a servant came into the hall carrying some beans. The green children brightened at the sight of these and signalled that they would like the beans to be brought to them. Even so, they tried to eat the stalks rather than the beans until they were shown otherwise. Once instructed, however, they seemed to relish the raw beans and would eat only those.

The boy, who, it became clear, was the younger brother of the girl, didn't thrive and died before long.

Because she learnt to eat different kinds of food, however, his sister grew stronger and eventually reached womanhood, her green skin slowly changing to a more mortal human colour. She also learnt to speak the local dialect and was able, over the years, to tell people a little about where she and her brother had come from.

They had led a strange existence in a twilight world called St Martin's Land. The people of that land venerated the saint and were, as far as people could judge, Christian. All the inhabitants were green, as the

girl had been when first found. There was no sun in the sky, she explained; the only light was like that at dusk in the normal world. From St Martin's Land they could see a bright country, but it lay across a huge river that effectively cut them off from any contact with the bright shining world across the water.

One day she and her brother were following their flock of sheep and had strayed a long way from home. After a while they became aware of a beautiful peal of bells. They followed the sound until, quite suddenly, they found themselves in the Suffolk countryside, dazzled by the strong sunshine and, understandably, very disoriented. They searched anxiously for the path that would lead them back home but couldn't see anything familiar. It was then that the men of Woolpit found them.

The girl, whose name seems not to have survived, stayed and worked as a servant for Sir Richard de Caine, until she married a local man and settled into the normal life of the village. The story of the two green children has been passed down through the centuries and remains an intriguing mystery. It is unusual among folk stories, in that it is never told as a conventional fairy tale but as an account of real events, even though they took place so long ago.

A few miles south of Woolpit a monstrous Black Shuck was believed to guard a hoard of treasure hidden at Clopton Hall in Rattlesden. This was a terrifying creature having the body of a monk and the head of a black dog.

In nearby Stowmarket there were claims of quite regular sightings of tiny people dancing and singing in the street, although whenever the little revellers realised

The spandrels of the original porch of St Michael's, Peasenhall featuring a dragon and a woodwose (lower right), reveal the fantastical imaginations of the 15th-century stone carvers

St Michael in Peasenhall is decorated with carvings recalling the time when pagan beliefs in fairies and mythological beings still had a significant following. The church porch displays two carvings opposite one another, a dragon and a woodwose. The latter was a wild man covered in hair and usually seen carrying a club. They were said to have been quite common in the vicinity.

Travel south down the Suffolk coast, past

they were being watched, they would quickly disappear. Some may find that the name of the street in question – Tavern Street – arouses a degree of scepticism about these claims!

In 1842, a man walking by some fields near Stowmarket, saw 'doll-like' people dancing in a ring. They looked insubstantial and wore sparkling clothes. Other people have claimed to see fairies in these fields.

Twenty miles east of Stowmarket, the church of

Aldeburgh and you come to Orford Castle, where a visitor as strange as the green children of Woolpit was once incarcerated. Ralph of Coggeshall, writing in the 13th century, tells a story about some Orford fishermen who caught a bald-headed man in their nets, whose naked body was very hairy and who couldn't, or wouldn't, speak even when tortured in the dungeon of the castle where he was kept. He ate raw fish and, when allowed to swim in the sea, he effortlessly dived under the nets placed to keep him from straying. He willingly returned, however, until one day came when he simply swam away, never to return.

Orford Castle on the Suffolk coast where the 13th-century folk tale tells of the trawling in by local fishermen of a 'fishman'

Looking east through the mists over the lake of Llangorse
toward the Nynydd Langorse range of the Black Mountains

Llangorse and the City Beneath the Lake

Fairies of south and mid-Wales

As the second largest natural lake in Wales, Llangorse is the setting for a number of Welsh fairy tales.

According to one legend, there is a lost city now covered by the lake, evoking memories of lost fairy realms that occur at several lakes in Wales. At Llangorse, the story runs that the land beneath the lake once belonged to a cruel and greedy princess. A poor man fell hopelessly in love with her and eager to exploit his passion to her own advantage, the princess agreed to marry him on condition that he brought her great wealth – acquired by any means fair or foul.

In order to satisfy his beloved's demands, the poor man robbed and murdered a wealthy merchant. All his plundered wealth was given to the princess, who kept to her side of the agreement and duly married the merchant's murderer. However, the merchant's spirit did not rest easy. It returned to warn the villainous couple that their crime would be avenged on the ninth generation of their family.

They ignored the ghost, however, and lived on into old age – old enough to see the ninth generation of their offspring enter this world. Then, one terrible night, a violent storm descended on the hills and mountains surrounding their home. Streams turned into torrents, torrents joined into waves and on all sides water cascaded down from the slope above, drowning the land below and all its inhabitants, leaving no trace of what had been there but covering the whole area with the waters of what we now know as Llangorse Lake.

*The legendary Glastonbury Tor at sunset topped by
the iconic 14th-century chapel tower of St Michael*

Glastonbury Tor ~ The Hollow Hill

Fairies of Somerset

Early Christians often used a dedication to the archangel Michael to sanctify a site long regarded as a centre for pagan religion. Glastonbury is no exception and atop the tor stands St Michael's church tower, the final remnant of the monastic settlement guarding its summit. Long before the chapel to St Michael was built, however, the lands below Glastonbury Tor were fretted with lakes, marshes and waterways with the tor rising out of them, mysterious, magical and serene. Even today, you can almost believe that the tor has once again become an island, when it is seen rising out of the misty landscape of the Somerset Levels.

The early inhabitants of the Summer Lands lived in lake villages and wended their way through the marshy land on hidden paths and wooden trackways, or by dugout canoe. It was they and their descendants who began to regard islands as sacred places and the stories they wove about them passed on to folklore.

This fairy kingdom, offering eternal youth in its glittering halls, was where the heroic dead were brought. The legend of King Arthur tells of him being

placed in a boat and being brought to Annwyn (or Avalon as it is called by his chroniclers) by beautiful, otherworldly maidens after he was fatally wounded at 'the last battle': the Battle of Camlann. And he's said to dwell still in the crystal halls of the Fairy King. Other legends use the Celtic name for Glastonbury Tor which was Ynys-witrin – the Isle of Glass.

Another story tells of the holy St Collen, who retired from his post as Abbot of Glastonbury in order to travel amongst his flock and preach to them. He became so weary of their godless ways, however, that he finally withdrew to live the life of a hermit in a rocky shelter on Glastonbury Tor. He didn't enjoy his quiet life of prayer and contemplation for long before he became involved in confrontation with Gwynn ap Nudd.

St Collen one day overheard two peasants outside his hermitage talking in hushed and reverent tones about the Fairy King. Hearing this, the holy man stormed out and berated them for believing in such superstitious, pagan nonsense. They warned him, in turn, against speaking so dismissively of the lord of Annwyn, in case he heard of it and was offended.

Collen retired back into his cell, no doubt to pray for the souls of the superstitious locals. Some time later there was a knock at the door and he heard a voice courteously requesting him to meet Gwynn ap Nudd on the summit of the hill. Collen refused and the messenger departed. He came back, however, the next day and again invited Collen to a meeting with the Fairy King. Again, the saint refused. On the third occasion the messenger delivered the invitation with a thinly veiled threat.

This time, the saint responded to the request and, leaving the safety of the hermitage, set out with considerable trepidation for the rendezvous on top of Glastonbury Tor. He was careful, though, to take with him a flask of holy water, which he hid in the folds of his robes. After labouring up the slope he reached the top, where he was amazed to see a beautiful castle. Collen could hear enchanting music and singing. Beautiful young men and women, seated on fine horses, rode out to meet him or strolled about the lawns of the castle. Collen was invited inside to meet the king, who sat resplendent on a golden throne. Gwynn ap Nudd seemed not at all angry with Collen for the disrespect he had shown earlier. In fact, he very courteously urged the saint to feast with him on the fabulous banquet spread out on tables in the royal hall. The Fairy King's generosity went further: Collen had only to ask, and any wish he made would be granted.

We do not know how tempted Collen might have been to accept the king's blandishments after living a life of denial and austerity. But while a weaker man might have succumbed to the the plentiful, exquisite food and wine on offer, Collen seized the flask of holy water from beneath his robes and quickly dashed the contents over the Fairy King and his Court. No sooner had the holy water touched the food-laden tables and the walls of the hall than the banquet and the castle vanished, the music ceased and the monk found himself alone on top of the tor with only the sound of the wind sighing through the grass.

These stories lie at the root of the local belief that Glastonbury Tor is hollow and that tunnels lead to and from it. Occasionally unearthly coloured lights are seen on the hill, a phenomenon that would only add to its eeriness and magical, fairytale reputation.

Perhaps Gwynn ap Nudd didn't vacate the hill after his confrontation with Collen, and his fairy realm and crystal halls may still lie there beneath the hill, imbuing the tor with a magical energy that continues to draw people to it to the present day.

Twenty miles west of Glastonbury and within a short distance of the sea at Bridgwater Bay, lies Wick Barrow, a bronze age burial mound, referred to locally as a pixie mound. One legend describes a farm labourer hearing a little voice like a child's complaining that its peel (a shovel used by bakers for putting bread in the oven) was broken. When he went to where the voice came from, the only thing he saw was a tiny peel, broken at the handle. He kindly mended it and put it back where he'd found it. He checked later to find it gone but in its place lay a delicious, freshly baked cake.

When the hill was excavated in 1907 archaeologists had considerable trouble recruiting manual labour to work on the dig; many local men felt it would be unwise to disturb the ancient ground. Those that were persuaded to dig thought they heard unearthly music and complained of becoming ill or experiencing bad luck afterwards. The discovery of the remains of a round, stone-built building clinched matters for the reluctant workforce – what else could it be, they reasoned, but the pixies' house itself?

South from Stogursey, across the Quantock Hills, fairy investigators will find St Agnes' Well at Cothelstone. This is a beautiful, healing well housed in medieval stonework. It was also used by lovers who would secretly visit the well on St Agnes' Eve (20 January) and tell the saint their sweetheart's name. If she was in favour of the match she would make it come about. You had to be careful, though, because pixies inhabited the place, too, and little offerings had to be left to dissuade them from causing mischief. The pixies still appreciate a pin being left as a gift by anyone

visiting the well.

Move further south, past Taunton, and the Blackdown Hills are rich in fairy sites. At the Holman Clavel Inn, Blagdon, 'Chimbley Charlie', a hearth spirit (also called a 'brownie'), lives over the fireplace and sits on a beam, or 'clavey' made of holly wood, or 'holman'. Once upon a time a local farmer made the mistake of scoffing at the story of Chimbley Charlie which he heard whilst supper was being prepared for him and his guests. His scepticism did not go down well with the resident sprite because when a maid, uneasy that Charlie might have been provoked, went to see if the farmer's meal was all right, she found his party's table had been cleared of crockery, cutlery and glasses which had all been returned to the cupboards by unseen hands.

Another Blackdown folk tale concerns a man from Combe St Nicholas who was riding home one day when he saw what looked like a fair or market taking place on the hillside near Pitminster. The strange thing was that all the people attending the fair were very

small and disconcertingly vanished when he passed through the crowd, only to reappear behind him. He also felt himself being poked and pinched by invisible hands. By the time he reached home he was in considerable pain and became paralysed down one half of his body. Other people have reported seeing the fair from a distance but have stayed well clear. It is also claimed that a fairy fair actually takes place regularly at Pitminster itself. The fairies will take money from pockets and leave worthless fairy money in its place.

A cobbler and his family living near Buckland St Mary in the Blackdown Hills shared their dwelling with a hobgoblin called Blue Burches. He loved to play tricks on the humans but they didn't seem to mind and often regaled people with stories about him. Eventually, much to their disgust, a priest came and exorcised him. Blue Burches duly vanished.

Buckland St Mary is allegedly the site where the pixies finally won a great battle with the fairies, who fled west, most of them settling in Ireland.

Cadbury Castle, at South Cadbury a few miles north of Yeovil, is popularly believed to be the site of the mythical Camelot, where King Arthur and his knights slumber beneath the ground, waiting for the call to come to Britain's aid once more. The magical doorway into the hill is said to open every seven years at midsummer.

Cadbury Castle was also said to have been used by fairies as a grain store, but they abandoned it when they heard the new church bells ringing. They left treasure behind in the hill but no mortal will find it as it retreats into the earth if anyone tries to dig it out.

~ON THE TRAIL~

Set high above the flat lands stretching in all directions, Glastonbury Tor seems a worthy crucible in which the ancient legends of St Collen and the Fairy King, of Avalon and King Arthur – and maybe even the Holy Grail itself – have been brought together to be preserved in folklore.

When viewed from the town of Glastonbury, the 14th-century tower of St Michael atop the tor stands sharp and austere against the wide Somerset sky; aloof and ancient it seems poised between heaven and earth. The tor lies a short distance from the town centre and although renovated paths have improved access, its steep flanks rise impressively as you climb towards the summit – but it is worth the effort. Once at the top, the views across Somerset, Dorset and Wiltshire are spectacular.

Visit on a misty day and what you lose in the view, you gain in mystical imaginings. Gazing out across the vista laid before you, it is not hard to envisage the mysterious watery realm evoked in Arthurian legend and so beloved of fairy lore.

Locations to visit

GLASTONBURY TOR:

The tor is to the north of the A361, just east of Glastonbury. It is signposted from Glastonbury town centre.

THE BLACKDOWN HILLS:

The hills lie to the south-west of Taunton, and south of the M5.

THE HOLMAN CLAVEL INN:

The Holman Clavel Inn
Culmhead, Taunton, Somerset TA3 7EA
Tel: 01823 421432

PITMINSTER:

The village is a few miles south of Taunton and south of the M5. A minor road leads to it off the B3170.

BUCKLAND ST MARY:

Buckland St Mary is just to the north of the A303 and about five miles due west of Ilminster.

CADBURY CASTLE:

The hill fort is reached via a small road off the A303 between five and six miles west of Wincanton. The road goes through the village of South Cadbury until it reaches the foot of the hill where a footpath leads up to the 'castle'.

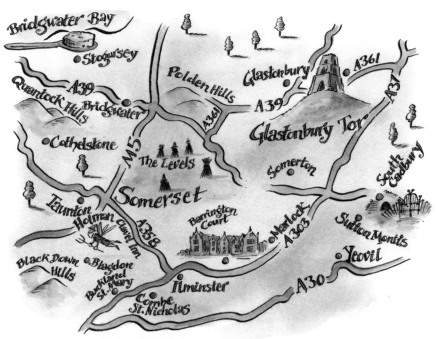

ST AGNES' WELL:

The village of Cothelstone lies down a minor road to the east of the A358 going north-west from Taunton. The turning is near the village of Bishop's Lydeard. The well is located in a field about 250 metres from Cothelstone Manor gateway and is reached through an iron gate by the roadside.

WICK BARROW:

The barrow is within the precincts of Hinckley Point Power Station, but is visible from outside the gates.

Bateman's, the secluded country home where Rudyard Kipling lived for over thirty years, and where he wrote Puck of Pook's Hill

Puck of Pook's Hill

Fairies of southern England

A century ago Pook's Hill in Sussex was known as Perch Hill and it owes its present name to an ancient belief in fairies and the inspiration they gave to the Nobel prize-winning author, Rudyard Kipling, after he moved to the Sussex countryside with his family in 1902. That was the year when Kipling and his wife, Carrie, bought a beautiful, Jacobean house called Bateman's near the village of Burwash. This was a quintessentially English country home and the Kipling family fell in love with it. Across the woods and fields, Perch Hill was just visible from the house, an enduring presence that steadily imprinted itself in Kipling's imagination.

One summer, Kipling and his two children, Elsie and John, used the small, natural amphitheatre of an old quarry near their home to act out a version of Shakespeare's play *A Midsummer Night's Dream*, in which fairies of course play a prominent part – in particular, a fairy called Puck.

This summer idyll and the almost Arcadian setting of his country home inspired Kipling to write a series of stories and poems, which he called *Puck of Pook's Hill*. In this, Kipling took Perch Hill as the model for Pook's Hill, where Puck, the best known of all sprites, is unwittingly called up by two children named Una and Dan. They, like Kipling's own children, perform a scene from *A Midsummer Night's Dream* in a fairy ring one Midsummer's Eve, which prompts Puck to appear in person. He takes them on a journey through time, meeting characters representing significant phases of England's history. After living at Bateman's for a few years, Kipling had become well versed in the history of the area and had come to know and love the surrounding countryside. The Sussex landscape around Pook's Hill and Bateman's is the starting point and background for the stories he wrote in what would become one of his most popular and enduring books.

William Shakespeare cast Puck as one of the leading characters in *A Midsummer Night's Dream*, portraying him as a comical, mischievous sprite, who delights in baffling the other characters with his magic and deceptions. This Puck is rather different from earlier versions of the well-known fairy.

In earlier traditions Puck was (at worst) a devilish creature or (slightly better) an impish nature spirit. He could change his shape and assume that of an animal. Sometimes he was portrayed as an old man, sometimes a sweet child, and yet again as a brownie or hobgoblin. His speciality was leading people astray, a talent that

Shakespeare uses to great effect in his play.

Kipling's Pook's Hill Puck is an altogether more helpful and obliging creature, though he is keen to dissociate himself from the gossamer-winged beings that were so popular with Victorian and Edwardian artists. He preferred to call his kind the People of the Hills, of whom he was the last, and he tells Una and Dan that he doesn't 'care to be confused with that painty-winged, wand-waving, sugar-and-shake-your-head set of imposters'. He distances himself further from such creatures, and many described elsewhere in this book, by being happy to have salt sprinkled on his biscuit, declaring:

'Some of us ... couldn't abide salt, or

horse-shoes over the door, or mountain ash berries, or running water, or cold iron, or the sound of church bells. But I'm Puck!'

South-west of Bateman's, in East Sussex, lies Herstmonceux Castle. It is well known that the Castle is haunted by the ghost of a drummer who fell at the Battle of Agincourt. A less conspicuous presence is that of a goblin said to guard a treasure chest in the Drummer's Hall.

Further to the west lie the South Downs and a number of fairy sites only a few miles from the Channel coast. Among them Chanctonbury Ring, near Washington, is an Iron Age hill fort steeped in legend. The Devil is said to appear if you run round the Ring seven times and it was a well-known haunt of fairies who liked to dance in the Ring on Midsummer's Eve.

Close by is Cissbury Ring, another favourite site for fairy revels at Midsummer. It is honeycombed with the shafts and galleries of Neolithic flint mines. Rumour had it that fabulous fairy treasure was concealed in a passage under the hill, but huge serpents attacked anyone who dared to try and find it.

A couple of miles away, Harrow Hill is the site of a late Bronze Age hill fort and Neolithic flint mines. According to legend it was also the last place inhabited by the fairy folk of England. Having lived there since the dawn of time, they were finally compelled to leave by the arrival of archaeologists, whose digging caused such a disturbance the fairies could tolerate it no longer and quit these shores for ever.

~On The Trail~

Bateman's was bequeathed to the National Trust by Rudyard Kipling's widow, Carrie, in 1939. As a fitting memorial to one of England's best-loved writers, the house has been kept just as it was in Kipling's lifetime and retains the essence of peace and timeless tranquillity that appealed to him when he first saw the tall-chimneyed house and felt 'her spirit – her Feng Shui – to be good'.

The lovely grounds, too, have been preserved as Kipling himself designed them. In his study is the large desk at which Kipling wrote *Puck of Pook's Hill*, amongst many other works. The desk is still cluttered with his bits and pieces as if the author has just got up from writing to walk around the garden and perhaps gaze across the treetops to Perch, or Pook's Hill. You too can follow in Kipling's footsteps and catch a glimpse of the Hill that inspired his well-loved tale and if you then take one of the paths winding through the beautiful grounds you will be led down to the River Dudwell, where you'll discover the restored, working watermill, which also featured in *Puck of Pook's Hill*. It is not hard to see how Kipling was so inspired by this perfect setting amidst the glorious Sussex countryside.

Locations to visit

BATEMAN'S:

Bateman's
Etchingham, East Sussex TN19 7DS
Tel: 01435 882302
Website: www.nationaltrust.org.uk

HERSTMONCEUX CASTLE:

Herstmonceux Castle
Hailsham, East Sussex BN27 1RN
Tel: 01323 833816
Website: www.herstmonceux-castle.com

CHANCTONBURY RING:

The hill is situated near the village of Washington, which lies on the A24 going north from Worthing. It can be reached on foot from car parks near Washington and Findon village.

CISSBURY RING:

The ring is near the village of Findon which lies on the A24 just north of Worthing. It can be reached on foot from a car park at the base of the hill.

HARROW HILL:

Harrow Hill lies on the South Downs north-west of Worthing, to the north of the village of Patching. It can be seen from several pedestrian rights of way in the surrounding area.

The wave-battered coastline at Zennor, famed for harbouring mysterious mermaids who are reputed to have tempted so many vulnerable Cornish fishermen

The Mermaid of Zennor

Fairies of far southwest England

For centuries the grey stone church of St Senara in Zennor has clung to its barren hillside withstanding the storms that roar in from the Atlantic Ocean to batter the gale-swept Penwith peninsula in western Cornwall. Below the village waves slop and splash around the coves at the base of the towering cliffs and inside the church is a reminder of the impact the sea has long had on the lives of the Cornish people. Although the church was heavily restored in 1890, one of its surviving medieval bench ends depicts its most mysterious visitor from times gone by: the fabled Mermaid of Zennor.

Dating from the 15th century, the carved wooden panel shows her with long flowing hair, holding a mirror in one hand and comb in the other: the quintessential mermaid of legends and sea shanties who lures men to an unknown fate beneath the waves. At Zennor, however, it was not a lovesick sailor who was seduced by the mermaid's beauty, but the leading member of the church choir: the handsome Mathew Trewella. Their story is told in varying versions, but one fact on which these agree is that for Mathew and the mermaid it was love at first sight.

According to one account the mermaid, named Morveren, daughter of Llyr, king of the ocean, was drawn to Zennor church by the beauty of young Trewella's singing voice. Dressed

The pew carving of the Mermaid of Zennor

as a human, with a woman's gown hiding her mermaid tail, she would struggle up to the church to join the congregation every night for the last hymn at evensong, which Mathew Trewella always sang. Alone at the back of the church, Morveren came and went without notice until one evening, after she had been attending evensong for almost a year, when she lingered longer than usual. She listened to Mathew singing one verse, and then another, and begin a third. Each refrain was lovelier than the one before, and Morveren caught her breath in a sigh.

It was only a little sigh, softer than the whisper of a wave, but it was enough for Mathew to hear. He looked to the back of the church and saw the mermaid with shining eyes and gleaming hair. His voice faltered at the sight of her and from that moment his heart was hers.

Morveren's father had warned that she was not to be seen by humans and in her panic she made her way back to the sea, with Mathew and other members of the congregation following her. In her haste, though,

she tripped and fell and Mathew Trewella saw the tip of her fish tail poking out from the hem of her gown. She warned that she was a sea creature and could not stay, to which Mathew replied, 'Then I will go with ye. For with ye is where I belong.'

So saying, he picked up Morveren and ran into the sea with her, never to be seen again by the villagers of Zennor. To be out of sight, was not to be out of mind, though. Mathew Trewella's voice continued to be heard by the fishermen of Zennor – singing soft and high if the weather was to be fine and low and deep if King Llyr was going to make the seas rough. From Mathew's songs, the fishermen knew whether to put to sea, or to stay in the safety of their anchorage at the foot of the cliffs.

An alternative version of the legend tells of a beautiful lady, richly dressed, with a lovely singing voice who occasionally went to church at Zennor. In this account Mathew Trewella, handsome again and blessed with a glorious voice of his own, determined to discover who the lovely stranger was after she smiled at him one Sunday. He followed her after the service as she made her way towards the cliffs and was never seen again.

Many years passed and Trewella's disappearance faded in local memory until the day when a ship's captain dropped anchor off Pendower Cove near Zennor. A short time later, the captain heard a voice calling from the sea. Looking over the ship's side he saw a beautiful mermaid with blonde hair streaming beside her, who asked him if he could move his anchor because it was blocking the doorway to her home. The mermaid was anxious, she explained, to return to her husband, Mathew, and her children. Fearful of mermaids and the bad luck they could bring ships, the captain promptly did as he was asked and moved away to anchor in deeper water, though he did return later to tell the people of Zennor the strange tale of Mathew Trewella and the mermaid.

It was to commemorate these events and to warn other young men of the dangers of associating with mermaids that the image of the Mermaid of Zennor was carved in the bench end in the village church.

The Penwith peninsula has land-based fairies to contend with as well. Hooting Cairn is a moorland hill topped with a striking outcrop of rock. From time immemorial it has had an eerie reputation and was given a wide berth by the locals. One dark night, two miners walking home from the tavern, a little the worse for drink, lost their way and found themselves near Hooting Cairn. The rocks began to fluoresce in the dark and emit weird sounds. Small things rustled in the

The eerie rocky outcrop known as Hooting Cairn

grass at their feet and they found themselves climbing closer to the hilltop, unable to resist. When they got there, fairies and pixies were gathered in a large circle round two figures wrestling with one another. Finally, one of the wrestlers was thrown down and mortally wounded. One of the watching miners was overcome with pity and prayed at his side. Immediately the scene before them dissolved and they were released from the spell, allowing them to run home as fast as they were able.

Geevor Tin Mine, down the coast at Pendeen, recalls the belief among Cornish miners that they shared their mines with 'knockers'. If you heard one of these small folk below ground, the tapping sound he made would lead to a rich vein of ore. They could be offended, however, especially by a miner whistling underground or by not sharing food with them,

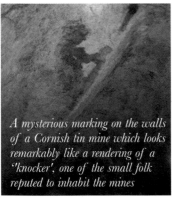

A mysterious marking on the walls of a Cornish tin mine which looks remarkably like a rendering of a 'knocker', one of the small folk reputed to inhabit the mines

as a miner called Tom Trevorrow found to his cost. Superstitious miners would leave little offerings of food for the knockers to keep them happy and, therefore, helpful. Tom was a sceptic and finally refused to carry on with this custom. That very day a fall of rock nearly killed him – as it was, his tools were buried beneath the rubble. From that time on, bad luck continued to dog Tom, until he was forced to give up his job as a miner.

Around the Cornish coast, eastwards past Land's End, Mermaid's Rock, lying off the pretty village of Lamorna in Mount's Bay, derived its name from a mermaid who frequented the spot and whose singing was said to foretell shipwrecks. The sweetness of her singing and the alluring sight of her combing her hair drew many fishermen to the rock and they, like Mathew Trewella, were never seen again.

A man from St Buryan, near Lamorna and Mousehole, William Noy, set out one night across moorland between Selena and Baranhaul Farms. He became lost and was drawn to lights and music. He entered an otherwordly gathering and was shocked to see his dead sweetheart, Grace Hutchens, playing a violin amidst little people dancing. She had been led to fairyland three years before, the time when she had apparently died. William attempted to rescue them both by turning his glove inside out, which he knew should break the spell. He lost consciousness and came to find that he was lying out on the moor, surrounded by concerned friends, who had been searching for him for three days. Grace was not with him and he never fully recovered from the grief of having lost her a second time. After a while, he died and was buried beside her.

Travelling in the opposite direction from Zennor, along the north Cornwall coast, brings you to Padstow and the treacherous sandbank known as Doom Bar, which lies off the entrance to the harbour at the mouth of the River Camel. There was a time when Padstow was an important port and a natural safe haven on an otherwise rocky coast. Under the care of a local 'merry maid' (mermaid), even the largest of ships were able to anchor at Padstow. That was until the day when the mermaid was fired at from a visiting boat. The shot missed. The mermaid dived under water for safety, but surfaced soon after to lay a curse. In her fury she vowed that Padstow harbour would be desolate from that day onwards. Not long after, a terrible storm struck the mouth of the Camel, wrecking several ships and throwing up the huge sandbank that became Doom Bar, where many ships have foundered over the centuries.

Another Cornish town to suffer a mermaid's wrath was Seaton, between Downderry and Looe. Once a prosperous fishing town, all that can be seen of Seaton today is a sandy beach that is said to have engulfed the town after a local man unwisely insulted a neighbouring mermaid and she responded by cursing his home town to be swallowed up by the sands.

The men of Lamorna, Padstow and Seaton would have been well advised, it seems, to have heeded the warning so graphically displayed for over 500 years on the bench end in Zennor church

~ON THE TRAIL~

There is no escaping the timeless awe of the sea when you visit Zennor. Standing on the majestic cliffs that surround the village, storm-blasted by the howling Atlantic, you can fully appreciate how this imposing landscape has been scoured by nature until the earth's very bones have been laid open to weather beneath the sun and the rain, turning grey and cracked with age.

It is also not difficult to see how, in a land and time where superstition carried greater credence than conventional wisdom, the sea should easily assume supernatural powers in men's minds, luring them to chance their luck with promises of love and fortune, then ensnaring them when they over-reached themselves.

On entering the church seek out the Mermaid of Zennor carved on the end of one of its ancient wooden pews. This crude but bold image of a mermaid with long, flowing hair, holding up her comb and mirror, though carved six centuries ago somehow still seems to capture how the congregation of that small community long ago regarded the unforgiving sea and its temptations – remaining as a warning to today's visitors and residents of Zennor not to underestimate the power and potentially fatal lure of the sea.

Locations to visit

ZENNOR:

The village lies on the B3306, to the west of St Ives.

HOOTING CAIRN:

Near St Just, close to junction of the B3318 and A3071, the cairn is highly visible and can be easily reached by public footpath.

GEEVOR TIN MINE:

Pendeen, Penzance, Cornwall TR19 7EW

Tel: 01736 788662

Website: www.geevor.com

MERMAID'S ROCK, LAMORNA:

Lamorna is reached by the B3315. The rock is in the cove

ST BURYAN:

The village lies on the B3283, which branches off the A30 a few miles south of Penzance.

PADSTOW:

Situated on the north Cornish coast, reached from the east via the A389 or from the south via the B3276 coast road.

SEATON:

On south Cornish coast on the B3247 a couple of miles junction with the A387 at Hessenford.

The misty shoreline at Vazon Bay where 'small men' from the fairy realm in England reputedly landed in search of beautiful wives

At War with the Fairies in Vazon Bay

Fairy folk on the island of Guernsey

With a wide expanse of white sand that slopes gently into the sea, Guernsey's Vazon Bay seems far removed from conflict and strife, but it is celebrated in Guernsey folklore as having been the battlefield for a very different kind of combat to that usually fought by mortals. Vazon Bay is the legendary setting of a battle between the human islanders of Guernsey and a force of fairies that landed there after sailing from their fairy realm in England. At the root of this violent confrontation, like many legendary battles, lay the power of love. And, like many legendary conflicts, this battle sent resonances echoing through the folklore and traditions of Guernsey until comparatively recently – as the story of Vazon Bay reveals.

It used to be said that Guernsey people tended to be on the small side. The reason for this, it was believed, was that most of them were descended from unions between the human inhabitants of the island and fairy folk, les petits faîtiaux. According to island tradition, these liaisons began when a beautiful young girl called Michelle de Garis was walking down a Guernsey lane one day and thought she saw something under the hedge beside the road. She stopped to look and found that it was a young man fast asleep. She gazed at him in wonder, because not only was he the handsomest man she had ever seen, but he was also smaller than any man laid eyes on before. This last fact didn't stop Michelle from falling deeply in love with him as she sat there enraptured. At last, the young man stirred and opened his eyes to find this lovely girl staring at him. It wasn't long before he was as much in love with Michelle as she was with him. Her family were suspicious of her suitor, correctly guessing that he came from fairy stock. She was so distraught by the thought of their marriage being forbidden that her father and mother relented and, with considerable misgivings, gave their consent to the match.

After the young couple were married they boarded a ship together and sailed away to live with the fairies in England. Before they left, the young groom

gave Michelle's parents a gift to show his gratitude to them for letting him take their beloved daughter as his wife. It was a bulb that grew into a beautiful flower, now called the Guernsey lily, which has become emblematic of the island.

Some time after Michelle and her husband left Guernsey, a group of islanders came down to the sandy white beach of Vazon Bay and saw a band of small men disembarking from their boats. It transpired that they had come from the fairy realm in England in search of beautiful wives like Michelle. The men of Guernsey were affronted by this and refused to let the fairies take the island girls away with them. A stand-off ensued, which escalated into a full-scale war between the humans and the fairy men. Despite their superior stature, the men of Guernsey lost and the fairies took the beautiful young Guernsey women to be their brides. Eventually, however, the fairies left their wives and sailed back to their homeland, but not before many had fathered children in Guernsey. This, it is said, is why their descendants were smaller than average. Tall islanders claim their descent from the few humans who survived the battle with the fairies.

There are fairy sites in different parts of Guernsey. The Fairies' Cricket Bat (La Longue Rocque to give it its proper name) at St Peter in the Wood, is the tallest standing stone on Guernsey. Not only did the fairies use it for playing cricket, but it acts as a fertility aid if touched by mortals. Older references call it The Fairies' Battledore. A fairy called Le Grand Colin fell out with his son when they were playing shuttlecock, stuck his bat in the ground and refused to play any longer – not a good loser.

The so-called Fairies' Hole, at St Peter in the Wood, is in fact the entrance to a Neolithic passage grave. Stories grew up amongst local people that it was the entrance to fairyland. Regularly, fairies would emerge from the entrance and dance on moonlit nights at the Trepied Dolmen on a nearby headland, Le Catioroc. This is also said to be the meeting place for witches and wizards. The French writer, Victor Hugo, claimed Le Trepied was haunted by the cries of women

The Fairies' Cricket Bat (La Longue Rocque)

waiting for their lover, the Devil.

L'Autel de Déhus is another passage grave that was also reputed to lead to fairyland and from which the little folk came out to play and dance when the moon was full.

Guernsey residents treated these sites with respect. When a local man demolished a passage grave to obtain stone for building, his friends were very apprehensive. He dismissed their fears as ridiculous, but when he drowned not long after, no one was really surprised.

~ON THE TRAIL~

Fairy invasions aside, Vazon Bay is a must if you like your beaches two miles long with white sand gently shelving to the sea. Here the eternal interplay between land and sea mirrors the ebb and flow of human events against the mythological backcloth that colours the history and folklore of this beautiful island. Stand on the beach in a tempestuous winter gale, give your imagination free rein and it is not too hard to conjure up a vision of Vazon Bay as a battleground between the unlikeliest of foes.

Wander through the shallows in bare feet on a balmy summer's day, however, and the tale of Michelle de Garis and her fairy lover comes more readily to mind. Gaze out to sea at present-day craft plying their way through the sun-dappled water and the arrival of a fairy bark gracefully easing its prow onto the soft white sand does not seem so remote. Beware though if it's steered by small, beautiful young men!

Locations to visit

VAZON BAY:

The bay is reached by the coastal road travelling up the west coast of the island and is about halfway along it.

THE FAIRIES' CRICKET BAT:

This menhir stands near the road to L'Erée, about a mile inland from Roquaine Bay.

FAIRIES' HOLE:

St Peter in the Wood is a little inland from Roquaine Bay, south-west Guernsey. Fairies' Hole (Le Creux es Faies) is by the Route de la Rocque.

L'AUTEL DE DÉHUS:

This burial chamber is near the north-east tip of the island, close to the village of Vale, on the Rue du Dehus.

Picture credits

Visit Scotland/Scottish Viewpoint 6, 7
Stock Scotland 10, 14
Mary Evans 9, 11, 17, 19, 27, 39, 40, 64, 65, 73, 77, 78, 87
Bridgeman 16, 23, 34, 35, 41, 55, 62, 69, 79, 84
Britain on View/Rod Edwards 18
Britain on View 22, 64, 68, 76
Britain on View/Joe Cornish 49
National Museums of Scotland 25
Isle of Man Government 30, 33
www.iomguide.com 33, 35
NTPL/ Mark Sunderland 38
Science and Society Picture Library 44, 45
Peter Ashley 52, 56, 57
Corbis 26, 54
Photo Library of Wales 60
Colin Ward 82, 85
John Stedman 83
Amanda Fraser 86
Adam Clutterbuck 90
Garden Picture Library 92
Guernsey Press and Star 93